Retire Early with ETF Investing Strategy

Early Retirement Planning Guide: How to retire early so you can quit your job, travel, and enjoy life!

Mark Kenna

Furthermore, the information that can be found within the pages described forthwith shall be considered both accurate and truthful when it comes to the recounting of facts. As such, any use, correct or incorrect, of the provided information will render the Publisher free of responsibility as to the actions taken outside of their direct purview. Regardless, there are zero scenarios where the original author or the Publisher can be deemed liable in any fashion for any damages or hardships that may result from any of the information discussed herein.

Additionally, the information in the following pages is intended only for informational purposes and should thus be thought of as universal. As befitting its nature, it is presented without assurance regarding its prolonged validity or interim quality. Trademarks that are mentioned are done without written consent and can in no way be considered an endorsement from the trademark holder.

Introduction

First, I would like to thank you for choosing *Retire Early with ETF Investing Strategy* and congratulate you for taking the first step to securing your future. Choosing an "out of the box" way to retire can be a scary step to take, but you are serious about your future and are willing to look at different options.

Choosing a retirement strategy that's not mainstream doesn't come without risk or worries. It's understandable since there isn't always a lot of easy information about it, but this book is here to help. Here you will find everything you need to know about planning for early retirement and investing in a little know thing called EFTs.

Together we will go through the information you need to know to successfully retire early, starting at the fact that you can retire sooner than you think. This will also help to convince you that retiring early can be a good thing. Then we'll move into the logical next step, and that's figuring out the money that you are going to need in retirement. There are a lot of people who get to retirement and discover they don't have enough money to live how they were before retirement. This is what scares a lot of people. But if you sit down and figure out what you are going to need, then you won't be hit by that unfortunate situation.

Then we'll move into looking at developing six income streams. That may sound like a lot of work, but not all of these are active income sources. Most will be passive income and things that you can continue even after retirement. This will ensure that you have the money you need to retire when you want, and the more money you have to invest, the more money you will have to live on.

Then we'll move into talking about investing, which is likely why you came here. We'll discuss what it means to be an income investor and how to figure out how much risk you are willing to take. Risk is a big player in investing and something that gets overlooked by inexperienced investors. If you risk more than you can afford, you are placing yourself in a bad situation that can't be easily undone. You have to know exactly what your risk is.

After that, we'll move into look at ETFs. ETFs aren't quite mainstream in the investing world. Most people choose the obvious investing choices, but those can get quite expensive, and some come with greater risk. This is why "thinking outside of the box" is a good idea with investing.

Once you understand ETFs, we'll come up with an accumulation plan for your ETFs and then the best ETFs to invest in. Ultimately, what you choose to invest in will be up to you and your risk, so you might do some more research and find other

ETFs that fit your profile better than the ones we discuss, and that is perfectly okay. It is your money and not mine.

Then we'll move into deciding if you want to live off of dividends or sell your investments when the time is right. You could also choose to do both, but we will look at that later on. Then we'll wrap things up with how you get to enjoy the rest of your life as a rich person. This will discuss the best practices for investing and retirement, as well as some frequent questions about ETFs to help improve your decision-making process.

While you may learn a lot of new terms and such in this book, some of which may be intimidating, you can retire early with this plan. If you trust my information and you take the time to budget, you will find success in ETFs and early retirement.

Chapter 1:Can I Really Retire Sooner Than I Think?

Early retirement seems like a fantasy to many, but it is possible to retire earlier than most. Most people retire between ages 66 and 70, but there are some who continue working. Then you have some people who have decided to take their lives into their own hands and retire before the age of 60. Early retirement has changed in meaning over the years.

Retiring early is no longer defined as the time when you choose to quit working forever. Instead, it is the moment when you don't have to actively work to earn money. But you are also free to continue working if you do something that you really enjoy. There is a huge difference in doing a job you love or a job that you can easily leave once you are tired of it because you have the flexibility and freedom of a person who planned and saved money.

There is scientific proof that working is good for a person, and most people who completely stop working begin to lose their mental faculties. It is even possible people who quit working altogether at an early age could die sooner. That means it might be best to see early retirement as a time when you choose to work because you want to and not because you have to.

We no longer have to live by the old school idea of once you retire you are done working. You can choose to do whatever you want when you retire, as long as it makes you happy.

You may still be wondering if it is worth the risk to retire early. I mean, with the lowered mental function if you do stop working completely, to possibly running out of money, who wouldn't question it. Let's look at five reasons why retiring early is a smart decision, and isn't as risky as people like to make it out.

1. Putting retirement off could end up being risky.

The first thing to think about when it comes to retiring early is that we don't know how long we are going to live, or how long we'll stay active and healthy. A lot of people end up hitting early retirement, not because they want to, but because they didn't have any other choice. They were either laid off, had a serious health problem, or had to start caring for somebody else. For this reason, along, it is a good idea to be more aggressive in saving up for your retirement so that you can get there on your own terms.

2. You completely despise your job.

If you really don't like your job, it might just be worth it to retire earlier than you had planned. Hating your job has a lot of implications for your mental and physical health, so it's not good to stick with something you hate. According to various studies,

20 to 40 percent of workers aren't happy with their jobs. When you don't like your job, you can end up suffering from sleep problems, weight gain, stress, and depression.

These same problems can also end up leading to irritability and fatigue. Not only that, but that unhappiness at work can spill over into your home life, causing you to be less happy in your marriage and create dysfunction within your family.

You should also know that retiring from the job that you hate doesn't mean that you have to give up work altogether. It could mean that you could go after a passion that you have always wanted to follow but weren't able to.

3. It is possible to be very productive during your retirement.

If you are worried that you are going to be unproductive and bored during your retirement, know that you can still do things even when retired. When you take a look at your retirement goals and savings, you may find that you can't quit working completely, but you could still be able to retire earlier than you thought and continue to work a bit, part-time.

If that's the case, you should look at finding something to do that is less stressful and more enjoyable. By generating some extra money this way will help your nest egg to last longer. If you like the job you currently have, you may be able to cut down to part-time can continue working there for a few more years. If you continue to work, if you only work 10 hours each week and make $12 an hour, you will still bring in an extra $500 each month. That little extra income each month will be able to cover some major expenses like food or utilities.

It's actually a good idea for a lot of people to continue to work some during retirement because jobs provide you with structure and gives you a chance to socialize.

If you don't want to continue working, you can be productive in other ways, as well. If you have made sure you will be financially secure, you can volunteer your time to organizations that you find important. If you are good at a trade or have a skill, you can offer lessons, such as language lessons or music. You could also start selling baked goods or crafts, or you can do some freelance work.

You can use all of your free time during retirement to improve your health as well. You won't be rushed anymore, so you can focus on fixing nutritious meals and take bike rides or long walks, or simply go to the gym on a regular basis. By getting healthier, you can enjoy your retirement years doing fun things.

You may even notice that your sleep has started to improve because you won't be faced with the stress of your job, and you also might not have to wake up as early.

4. You can easily prevent yourself from running out of money using annuities.

A lot of people steer clear of early retirement because they believe they have to have a stockpile of money to make sure they don't run out. There are several ways to prevent this, but one way is to spend some of your retirement money on some fixed annuities. This is like buying yourself a pension income that you can depend on. It gives you the ability to set yourself up to get a monthly check and even some that you adjusted for inflation.

5. It isn't worth delaying your Social Security.

Lastly, you could be putting off retiring because you know that each year past the full retirement age that you delay collecting your benefits, they will go up by around eight percent. You also may be aware that collecting early, which you can start at 62, creates a smaller check.

What you might not know is that delaying isn't that easy of a decision. Even the Social Security Administration explained this by stating that if a person were to live to the average life expectancy, you are still going to get the same about of money no matter if you start receiving at 62 or at the age of 70. While you may get smaller checks when you collect early, you will receive more of them. You can use that money to invest in stocks as well.

This means that retiring early could be more within your grasp than you may have thought. At the very least, you could retire a few years earlier than previously believed.

The best way to make sure you can retire early is to come up with a retirement strategy. Any good investment strategy should be a simple one that focuses on real estate, bonds, and stock, and to make sure it is executed consistently. You need to have short-term investments, which is money you will want to have within five years, and long-term investments, which last ten years or more.

While you are free to invest in whatever you want to, you should only invest in things that you understand and stick with assets that have done well historically. You also want to make sure that your money is working as hard as it can by making sure it is invested in a tax-efficient way. And all that means is that you invest in your accounts correctly. Throughout the rest of the book, you will learn about these things to ensure you get the most from your investments and retirement.

Chapter 2:Determine What You Want and Need Your Retirement Money For

You have made the decision to retire early, so the first thing you have to do is to plan for retirement. One part of that is figuring out how much money you are going to need. The road to retiring early takes discipline to invest, save, and earn all you can.

Early retirement is different for everybody, so what yours is going to look like it is going to be determined by what you need. We will look at the general steps you are going to need to take to reach early retirement, and then you can change them up to make them work for you.

Take An Inventory

The first thing you need to do is to take an inventory of your finances right now. There are two things that you must figure out, and that is your net worth and your annual spending. Both can be figured out with a little math. For the annual spending, you can get a good guesstimate by looking at your credit card statements and all of your checking account habits. It would probably be in your best interest to start semi-automated tracking using an app to keep up with the amount of money that you spend each year.

To figure out what your net worth is, because everybody has one, all you have to do is subtract your liabilities, the things you owe, from your assets, the things you own. Don't confuse your net worth with your income. Your net worth is one figure that represents what your financial standing its. This figure could be positive or negative, big or small. While a lot of people love the sound a $1 million net worth, there isn't the right number. Most people will find that their net worth increases as they age.

More importantly, having a high income doesn't necessarily mean that you are going to have a high net worth. In 2016, it was found that the typical American family had a net worth of $97,290.

The first thing you need to do is list out all of your assets. Write down whatever you have that is of substantial value. While you do need to include intangible things, like investments, you do not put your salary here. Income is cash flow and not net worth. Assets you would include are the value of your home, vehicles, cash value of a life insurance policy, balance in retirement accounts, investment accounts, savings accounts, and checking accounts. You could also include the cash value of things like expensive clothing, furniture, art, and jewelry, as well as business interests.

Then you will list out all of your debts. This is everything you own to lenders and creditors like mortgages, loans, credit cards, and tax liability. Then you will take your liabilities and subtract them from your assets. Now you have your net worth, but that is simply a snapshot. If you are making payments on your debts or adding to a savings account, this number is going to increase. It can also decrease as well, so be careful.

As far as annual spending is concerned, all you can do is looking through your bank statements to see how much money you spend each year. And it is a good idea to save up about 25 times your annual spending.

Figure Out Your Target Number

Once you have an outline of your early retirement, you have to figure out how much money you are going to need to make it happen. As mentioned above, most early retirees say it is a good idea to have 25 to 30 times your expected annual expenses invested or saved. Once you figure out your target number, you can then break it down into monthly, weekly, and daily savings goals.

This is part of the process that you might find a bit difficult to do on your own, especially when you are looking at multiple scenarios, such as a recession that could affect investments. Finding a good financial planner to help you crunch your numbers and provide you with an actionable plant can help you to reach your goals. They can also keep you accountable if you want them to.

Hopefully, you will be close to paying off all of your debts by the time you do retire, so that would mean that you have more money to use just for living.

To start figuring out your target number, look at your current monthly spending and think about what numbers will lower, what might increase, and what you may add or eliminate. Once you have figured out your final monthly expense, multiply that number by 12, and now you have your annual retirement needs. To make that number even better, I would recommend increasing that number by 10 to 20 percent. This will ensure some wiggle room.

There are two things that people tend to overlook when coming up with this number, and that is health care and taxes. Both of these can end up bringing your early retirement to an early end. Health coverage will be covered later, so we get to talk about taxes. Your goal should always be to minimize them. In order for that to happen, you are going to want to strategize about how and when you pull income from investment accounts.

Alright, now you need to figure out your savings needs. Let's say that you figure out that you spend about $60,000 a year, and that's factoring is some wiggle room. To make sure you are well prepared, you will want to make sure you have at least $1,500,000 saved. That is 25 times your annual needs, which is what I mentioned earlier. This rule also assumes that your retirement nest egg has also been invested so that it will continue to grow. If it's not, then you will likely be out of money in 25 years.

That also brings us to a second rule. The four percent rule. This means that you are allowed to withdraw four percent of your invested savings in the first year of your retirement. In the following years, you will draw out that same amount once it has been adjusted for inflation.

The rule comes from research done in the 1990s that tested various withdrawal strategies against historical information. You may decide to take a more or less conservative approach, depending on the investments you make, risk tolerance, and the way the market is performing.

Change The Way You Are Spending Now

You will find it hard to build long-term wealth if you are constantly spending more money than you are making. If you want to retire early, it is very important that you start to live below your means as this is the best way to invest and save aggressively.

The main places you need to look when it comes to reducing your expenses are food, transportation, and housing. This can go quite a long way to increase your savings. Depending on the amount of money that you spend, you will want to aim for one of three types of early retirement: fatFIRE, leanFIRE, and FIRE.

FIRE stands for financial independence, retire early, and it is a numbers game.

LeanFIRE would be a person who has saved 25 times their annual expenses, which means that they have lived off of a "lean" budget, and will spend less than average Americans. But, a person who reaches fatFIRE will spend more than most. Regular FIRE would be a person who is spending in line with the average of Americans.

According to Census data, the average American household spends around $61,000 each year. For the regular FIRE person, they will continue to spend that amount after retirement. LeanFIRE would spend less than that after retirement and fatFIRE, would spend more. If you don't plan on embracing frugality in retirement, then you would fall under fat fire. But if you are a simple Midwestern couple, then you would likely be considered a leanFIRE. All of this will play a part in the previous step of figuring out your numbers.

Leverage The Income Your Make

It is very important that you keep all of your spending in check, but you will only be able to cut costs to a certain extent. A bigger difference can be made by increasing the income you are currently making. To cut your daily spending and expenses takes a constant and consistent effort, and is a short-term solution, but increasing your flow of cash is a long-term solution.

It is a good idea to start a side hustle to help diversify all of your income. The most lucrative ones tend to be passive incomes, like real estate. Coming up with a passive income source to cover your monthly expenses will provide you with more flexibility. We will discuss these sources in the next chapter.

Max Your Retirement Accounts

In nearly every story about financial independence, you will hear a common strategy: frequent and early savings. Typically, one of the best ways to improve your savings is to have retirement accounts.

IRAs and employer-sponsored retirement plans will provide you with unparalleled investment growth and tax advantages. Right now, you can add $6000 to a traditional IRA and $19000 pretax to a 401(k) that you can get a tax deduction.

There is a caveat to stuffing retirement accounts as full as you can when you are planning on retirement, and that is the restrictions on withdrawals. You aren't allowed to remove money from your 401(k) before the age of 59 and a half without a penalty. However, you are able to dip into your Roth IRA, which you fund with after-tax money and take out your contributions tax-free whenever you want.

Invest What You Have Left Over

Once you have maxed out your retirement accounts, you should move over to brokerage accounts. This money you will invest directly into the stock market, and then you can cash out whenever you need to. We'll talk about investing in ETFs later on.

Work To Pay Off Your Mortgage

When you are preparing to retire early, an obvious move is to eliminate high-interest consumer debts, but paying off a mortgage early isn't always so cut-and-dry. Some people see being liability-free is a good idea, but others see the money saved in interest payments pale to the possible investment returns.

Look At Your Health Insurance Options

When you leave your full-time employer, it means you are also saying goodbye to employer health insurance. If you plan on waiting for 65 to roll around to get Medicare, typically, the best option would be to join a working spouse's employer plan, if that option is available to you.

Otherwise, you should look at getting continued coverage through your former employer under COBRA, through possible subsidies with the Affordable Care Act, health-sharing plans, or having a part-time job.

Come Up With A Backup Plan

No matter how much planning you put into place or how foolproof the plan may be, you still need to think about what could go wrong. What if you discover that you don't like the unstructured days of retirement, would you decide to go back to work? What would happen if the economy tanked and it takes your net worth, would you be able to cut expenses? Going through some worst-case scenarios is a good way to make sure you are ready for anything.

Once you have your plan figured out, it is time to start putting that plan A into action. But as you are doing that, you have to make sure that you continue to enjoy your life right now. You need to make sure you save and invest, but you can't forget how to live in the present.

Chapter 3:Develop and Income Stream From 6 Sources, Not Just One

The next thing you need to do is to start diversifying your income. I know hearing the number six for how many income sources you should have sounds big, but I'm not asking you to have six jobs you have to split your time between. Instead, a lot of what diversifying your income involves are passive income sources, which are things you aren't actively working on each day. Some researchers have found that millionaires, on average, have seven income streams.

You may be wondering if the extra income streams are what made the millionaire or if it was the other way around. While seven may not be a magical number, it does seem that these two concepts on two sides of a coin. It could be that multiple income streams made the millionaire, but it is also true that millionaires simply understand how important it is to have multiple income streams.

The goal of coming up with several income streams is to maximize potential in the different categories you have available. Since you are just starting out, you can't really expect that you are going to generate a bunch of income. However, if you make sure that you are maximizing your income potential through your main salary, you will discover that you have excess income that you will be able to reinvest in other income streams so that you can earn even more money.

We looked at net worth earlier, and that is another goal of these income streams. You want to increase your net worth as much as you can while you are still actively working. The more your net worth is, the better your retirement is going to be.

I mentioned that most of these are passive income streams. I want to take a moment and explain what that means. Active income is the money you make from jobs you have to actively go to and work, such as your office job. If you don't do anything at that job, then you won't get paid.

Passive income is making money from something that isn't directly related to active work. Dividends and interests are two examples of passive income. Most of these passive income sources will require active work at first that you make a little bit of money for, while most of your income will come later.

You shouldn't think that passive income doesn't require any work. You will still have to do some work. It just means that the income you make isn't directly tied to the hour many hours of work you put in.

We are going to look at some of the most common income streams that you can get started in. Of those, you simply need to pick at least five to start, since you already have your primary income source. While it may sound like a lot of work, having these extra income sources will allow you to save up more money faster than if you simply had your main source of income.

There are a few things you want your other streams of income to be. First, you want it to be flexible. Ideally, you want to be able to call the shots when it comes to time, especially if you a full-time job. Second, you want it to be scalable. You want to find income sources that have, at the very least, the chance of creating a lot of income. Third, you want it to be sustainable. You want your secondary money sources to be able to generate money for you even when you are aren't actively working. Lastly, you want them to be enjoyable and inexpensive. You don't want your secondary sources of income to cost you money or create more stress for you. The goal is to ease your financial woes and not to make them worse.

Primary Salary

Your primary salary is likely your main income stream. This is where everybody starts, and it is most likely your full-time job. The goal here is to try and maximize this salary so that you can start generating the free cash you need to invest it into other income streams.

How is this done? Well, you will want to try to get as high of a paying job as you are able to. Ask your boss for a raise. Use sites like glassdoor.com to see if your salary competes with the same job at other companies. There are some companies that force their workers to leave just to get a raise and then return for another raise. This is a very common strategy, and it just might work for you.

There is also another theory about this primary salary. You could try to generate enough to have a little bit of extra cash flow, but you work at a place that is stress-free and have some time to dabble in different projects. If you have the means to do so, having a startup is one way to do this.

Either way, the main perk of this primary salary is that it normally provides you with benefits like insurance, which can help to protect you as you are pursuing your other income streams.

- Secondary/Spouse Salary

I don't count this as another income stream for you. Instead, this is secondary to your primary. No matter what you plan on undertaking, it is important to have a team. Teamwork can help you in a variety of ways, even if it is simply bouncing new ideas off of somebody else. For most people, this is going to be your spouse. If you have a spouse, then the two of you should bring your primary incomes together and maximize them.

Investment

The first option you have, after employment, is to find diversification through investing, which is a logical step that most people take. It is very important that you look at the reasons why you want to invest because, at some point, you are going to be using that money for something. In this case, your reason is likely for early retirement. But when it comes to investing, it isn't all about storing money away for a rainy day, that's what having an emergency fund is for. Investing means you have the capital to generate income.

Look at it this way, when you're saving for retirement, you want to save enough in your investments to create enough income to replace your main salary. Let's say your primary salary makes you $50,000 each year. To be able to create $50,000, you are going to need nearly $1,700,000 saved up, and then be able to create three percent cash flow on that.

If needed, you can also draw down on your principal, but this is a return of the invested capital, and if you were to continue doing this over a long period of time, you could end up using up all of your resources.

Rental Property

Another very common way for a person to make extra money is to purchase a rental property. This is a lot like investing in that you will need a sum of money to purchase another piece of property, and then that property gives you money through rent. There are expenses that you will have to take care of, which are different from investing, and these include things like taxes, utilities, mortgage, and so on. This will all have to be considered when you calculate the return on the rental property.

There are tax advantages to having rental properties that you don't get with investing. The main problem with having a rental property is that that initial capital that you need to get started. Most people that are starting to diversify their income aren't going to have a 20% down payment in order to buy property. This is typically why this is done later on.

However, you have some options to doing this earlier, like looking into real estate crowdfunding. Real estate crowdfunding gives you the chance to become a limited owner in real estate, and you don't need as much money to start. This is a good option for getting started in real estate.

The site RealtyMogul gives you the chance to get started in real estate for as little as $5,000. You will have the option of commercial and multi-family properties to invest in. Fundraise is another platform you can try. You only need $500 to get started, and they offer several different options.

If you have a little more money than that, you could try Roofstock. They give you the chance to buy a single-family turnkey investment online.

Some people like to try out house flipping, but this can be very risky. You are going to not only need the money to buy the house, and the credit to do so, but you will need funds to fix the house before you can try to sell it. That's the thing with house flipping that you sell the house once you are done, and don't rent it out.

House hacking is also another option. This is similar to owning rental properties. This is simply where you leverage the house you currently live in as a rental. This could mean renting a room or setting up an Airbnb listing.

Hobby or Online Business

Another common income stream is to create a side business. You could make this business offline or online, and I like to refer to them as a "hobby business" because it typically gets created from a person's hobby. For example, if you are a techie person or like working online, you could sell things on eBay or simply create your own website. You can also promote your own services online with sites like Fiverr.

If you would to work offline, you could start working with something like Partylite Candles, Avon, or any other various jewelry and clothing lines.

Some people will also choose to write an eBook since anybody can be an author on Amazon nowadays. Writing the book is the simple part, making actual sales in a different story and takes a lot of work.

If you are good at photography, you can also sell stock photos. There are a lot of different websites where you can do this. Fredigitalphotos.net and 123rf.com are a couple of options.

You can also choose to offer a service instead of an actual product. If you have a skill set that people could pay you for, then this a good option. Some common things people pay for are lessons in music or language, writing, social media management, babysitting, tutoring, consulting, coaching, and resume help. This is a great option because you get to set your own hours and price, but it can also take a while to create a client list.

Be A Micro-Entrepreneur

I think this is different than selling a service or product. This is a side hustle, but you have the freedom to choose when you want to do it, but you aren't faced with having to start your own business. The first option would be to start driving for Uber or Lyft. Ride-sharing is one of the side hustles that you are able to do, truly, 100% on your own. You get to choose when you drive. The only thing you will need is a new-ish car and some spare time.

Another option is to deliver for Uber Eats or DoorDash. If you don't like the thoughts of having strangers in your car, then you could simply deliver food to stranger's houses. Again, you are free to choose when you do this during the day.

Coming Up With Several Income Streams

The point is that you need to diversify your income in several different ways to help you retire early. You don't have to get all of your income streams up and going at once. Pick the first one you think you can start right now, and begin with that one. Then continue to add another income stream as you can.

There a some of these options that don't require you to have a bunch of money to start with. All of them will require some time to get started, though. You can simply continue to work, invest excess income, save up a bit to get a rental property or rent out a room in your house, and then start an online job without having to break a sweat.

When it comes to coming up with your passive streams, they aren't all created equal. The stock market is the only passive income stream where you bear all of the risks and get all of the rewards. In all other cases, you have more risk than the rewards you could possibly get because other people may be involved.

Chapter 4:Become An Income Investor

Income investing is a strategy to help you build wealth that involves coming up with an asset portfolio that will provide payouts that you can depend on. This means, for most, gathering a collection of high-quality bonds and dividend-paying stocks that they can count on as a cash source that requires little work from them. Having a well put together portfolio of various stocks and bonds is a rewarding and accessible route to creating a decent stream of "passive income."

There are some people who believe that income investing can only be done by retirees and older investors, and there are a lot of good reasons for this association. However, having investments that are income-generating is a valuable financial avenue for those of any age. Dividend-paying stocks often outperform those that aren't, and a safe choice is quality bonds because they can help your wealth preservation, and they can prevent your purchase power from being eroded. This means that you should think narrowly when it comes to who should and should not become income investors.

The best makeup of your portfolio is going to depend on what you want to achieve and how much risk you are willing to take. Because of this, you should make sure that you understand all of the various forms of assets that can help you create an effective portfolio, some characteristics and metrics to be on the lookout for a while evaluating items, and an idea of what you goals are so that you can figure out the holdings and strategies that fit your needs.

Income investing was born from social unrest during the 20th century. Despite all of the nostalgia of the time, society was actually really messy. It was messy in the fact that Irish and Jewish people weren't able to get hired, and if you fell into the LGBTQ category, you were signed up for electroshock therapy. Black women and men were always faced with the threat of rape or a mob lynching. Everybody thought Catholics were being controlled by the pope. If you were female, you wouldn't get hired for anything other than typing, for which you only got paid a fraction of what men did for the same work. They also didn't have company pension plans or social security, which resulted in most elderly people to live in abject poverty.

But why did this cause income investing? These types of circumstances caused the rise in income investing simply in order to survive. Unless you were a well-connected white man, decent pay was out of the question. The main exception was if you owned stocks and bonds in Pepsi or Coca-Cola. These types of investments didn't care if you were young, old, white, black, male, female, or whatever. You were sent interest and dividends during the year, depending on your investment and the company's performance. This is the reason why it became a rule that as soon as you had earned some money, you need to save it and invest it. They didn't trade stocks during that time. They invested and forgot about it.

Now, let's move to look at different aspects of income investing.

Bonds

Bonds are a type of investment known as fixed-income, which means that they will give you a certain amount of money during a specified time period. When you buy a bond, the money you pay for is basically a loan to the company or government. Once you have reached the end of your agreed-upon loan period, which is called maturation, the bondholders will be able to cash in their bond and get its principal value. How much interest that your loan will generate will all depend on the length of its maturation and the risk of the default.

You have two main types of bonds you can invest in:

- Government:

These bonds are basically money that you loan a certain government that will provide you with a certain amount of interest every year. Bonds for the US are typically seen as the safest choice because the US government has, historically, been a stable government. There are some government bonds that provide you with special tax advantages, like a tax-free municipal bond.

You can also choose a foreign bond. However, depending on which country it is for, there can be a bigger risk of not receiving the principle once you reach maturation, or never getting your principal value back. If the foreign government decides not to make good on the bond, it is often very hard to get restitution since you probably won't have access to their court systems.

- Corporate:

These bonds have pretty much the same setup as a government bond, but there are some differences that you should be aware of. As you would guess by the name, these bonds are simply loans given to a company at a specified amount over a certain period of time. Much like with government bonds, depending on the risk, the interest will be higher or lower. As opposed to government bonds, corporate bonds normally have to be bought in 1000-bond lot.

A lot of people think bonds are safer than dividend stocks, but this might not always be true. If you choose a bond with a high-interest rate, that will normally be because there is a higher risk that the company or country won't pay back your loan. Those who provide a high yield but also have a really high risk of defaulting will often be called "junk bonds." Investors have the

option of using the bond rating from a third-party site to assess
how likely it is that your principal will be repaid.

Dividend Stocks

When it comes to stocks, you are basically buying a part of a
company. The shares that you buy will generate a part of the free
cash flow and earnings of the company. Not every company will
send money straight to those who hold stock, but the ones that
choose to do so are called "dividend stocks."

Dividends provide companies with a way to give their
shareholders money. These are normally paid out of their free
cash flow, which is figured out by subtracting the capital
expenses from their operating cash. Companies can also choose
to use their cash piles, or if they have to, take out debt to pay
their dividends, but investors don't typically like these methods
of funding.

Besides purchasing single stocks that pay dividends, investors
can also buy mutual funds or ETFs. ETFs are basically securities
that have been bundled together and then purchased on a
trading exchange. Mutual funds are another type of security that
bundles together bonds, stocks, and other assets, which are
actively managed and purchased from a broker or fund
manager.

Certificate of Deposit

CDs are another fixed-income type of investment that works a lot like a savings account or a bond. Your money isn't loaned to a company or government, and is, instead, given to a ban. Then longer of a term you choose, the better your interest rate will be.

Rates that you can get on these investments are often going to be lower than bonds that are held for a comparable time, but these to have a greater upside in that they are insured by the FDIC for a max of $250,000. This means that even if the bank goes belly up, you will still be able to get back your principal.

The low-yield, low-risk investment makes CDs perfect for retirees who are looking to preserve the money they have and allow it to grow and offset the effects of inflation. However, if you try to remove the money before the specified date, you will be faced with a penalty.

Payout Ratio

The payout ratio for a company is the percentage of its free cash flow or earnings that is put towards covering their dividend distribution. You can find these ratios by dividing the FCF and the complete amount of dividends that the company will distribute during a given year. If a company has a payout ratio over 100%, that means they are making less cash than what they have to payout on dividends, and that means they will likely have to take out debt or use cash assets in order to pay. This is normally an unsustainable dynamic and tends to signal that a suspension or dividend cut is getting close.

Companies with low ratios tend to have a bit more leeway with their dividends, but they could end up having other needs that can end up preventing them from giving a big payout.

Payout Growth

The payout growth is basically how much a company has been able to increase its payouts per share over a certain time period. The growth rate can be figured out by taking the dividend at the close of a certain period, subtracting the value of the dividend at the beginning of your comparison period, and dividing that number from the start of your comparison period.

If a company were to repurchase the stocks or retire some of the shares, it would reduce how many dividend-generating shares it has. This would mean that buybacks would give the company a chance to increase how much dividend they would pay per share over a specific time without having an increase in their total distribution because there won't be as many shares receiving payments.

Dividend Yield

This is a certain percentage of a company's yearly payout that is represented by a percentage of the price of its stock. You can find yield by dividing the annual dividend with the price of the stock.

If you bought a stock for $50 a share and it pays out a dollar each year, its yield would be 2%. That means if you bought 50 shares, you would get the equivalent to a value of a share in through the dividends in a given year. Depending on what payment option you choose, you could get $50 in income or get an additional share for your holding through a reinvestment (DRIP). Investors tend to end up owning fractional shares because of being a part of a DRIP program, and the fractional shares are still going to pay your dividends, and you can sell them just like full shares, provided that you are operating your stocks through a brokerage.

Dividends tend to be paid out according to the company's schedule. Most choose to pay on an annual, quarterly, or biannual basis, but there are some who will pay monthly. Some companies will provide a special dividend, which is a payment that is unscheduled and does not repeat.

Taxes and Dividends

Most of the time, your dividend payouts are going to be taxed at the rate of 15%, but this tax rate could go from zero percent to 20%, depending on various situations. If you have a DRIP account, you are still going to have to pay taxes. If you own 100 shares with a two percent yield, and you reinvest the $200 in the payouts through a DRIP, you are still going to be taxed on that $200 even though you reinvested it.

You can minimize this by shifting the timing of the taxation to work for you, which most people do through IRAs. The downside would be that you have to leave the money in them until the age of 59 and a half, or you will have to face fees, but they still make helpful tools. You have two options for IRAs, Roth and traditional.

With traditional IRAs, the taxation of the funds you add to the account is deferred. When funds are added to the IRA, you will be able to take a deduction from your taxable income and is a great way to reduce the taxes you owe. However, your withdrawals will be taxed normally. Most people will often generate less income during retirement, so pushing the taxation until after you retire could mean that it is taxed at a lower rate.

When it comes to Roth IRAs, you have to pay taxes on the money that is added to the account during the year that you add it, but it won't be taxed again when it is withdrawn. This makes a Roth IRA useful for investors who are income-focused and still have several years before retirement because it gives dividend payments a chance to accumulate.

Dividend Growth Investing

Dividend growth investing will require you to select stocks that have rapidly growing payouts, even if they don't offer great yields. This is done with the understanding that you will be able to build to have a bigger yield with time. Some stocks could look like they have a small yield if you were to compare it to an S&P 500 index average yield. However, if that company raised its payout annual by 15% over five years, the yield will have doubled by the end of that time period.

Companies will huge dividend payouts often grow earnings at a slower rate when compared to the market, and it tends to deliver smaller payout increases. Meanwhile, companies that make earnings at a faster rate than older companies in industries such as industrials or telecommunications are able to provide you with fast growth in dividend. Dividend growth stocks are able to provide you with a better balance between a growing returned income and an increase in stock price than the ones who already have bigger yields.

How Important are Payout Growth Streaks?

You should always look at finding companies that, historically, has delivered a consistent payout growth each year. Companies that cut dividends often means that they are not doing well, and when they consistently have increases in dividends mean that there will be a continued growth in payouts.

After a company has been able to create a multi-decade streak of consistent payout growth, dividend growth will become an expected part of owning a stock. The company will be able to count on the backlash from their shareholders if it doesn't give them the increase in payouts, or if they cut their dividends. You want to look for companies that have proven their self to be sturdy and can thrive over a long period of time, but shareholder expectation is also able to encourage a company to continue to grow their dividends during slow periods or recessions.

Chapter 5:How Risky Can You Be? Come Up With The Right Mix of Stocks, Bonds, Real Estate and Cash

Investing isn't something that works the same for everybody. Everybody is in it for various reasons. All of your personal and retirement goals have a lot to do with the way you choose to manage your investments.

Depending on what you want to do in retirement or what you would like your investments to do for you, it is going to change your decision-making process and your risk-management strategies. It is very important that you understand what your goals are. The more you understand them, the better your chances are to reach them.

Making sure that you consistently achieve your goals will make you a better and more successful investor. You can't make any stock purchase without there being some risk. Investors take risks because it gives them a chance to succeed. But with each stock, you have different types of risks, and those different risk levels can vary widely. So how much risk should you take? I can't answer that for you because, once again, everybody is different. It will all depend on how much risk you can afford.

Risk tolerance is basically how much exposure to loss you are okay with. It's basically how much money you are willing to lose trying to reach that big payoff, and long you may be willing to wait to get your money.

Another term you will hear is risk-reward. Risk-reward is the trade-off that lies under nearly anything that can generate a return. Whenever you invest money into something, there will be some sort of risk that you might not actually get your money back. For facing that risk, you can expect a return that compensates you for your possible losses. Basically, the bigger your risk, the more you should get back for holding that investment, and the smaller your risk, the less you will get.

How much risk you are willing to take will determine how fast you will reach your goals, or if you ever meet them. If the goals you have involved a short timeframe, it may not be a good idea to play it safe. For a person who has a modest goal and few decades to work that "slow and steady" approach, that may be the best option.

The first thing you need to do is to start by looking over your investing goals. Are you going to be able to reach your goals by slowing growing your money over several years? Do you have very lofty goals that are going to need big gains?

Also, you need to remember that various portfolios will be able to handle various levels of risk. If you have a large and carefully

45

diversified portfolio, then it will typically rebound from loss caused by a risky investment, but a smaller portfolio could completely fall apart by too many risks or simply a single big risk.

For example, let's say there are two portfolios. One of them has $25,000, and the other has $250,000. Now, if they both lost $1,000, it would cost them $25,000 portfolio four percent, but the other portfolio would lose only 0.4%. If they both lost $10,000, that would be 40% for the $25,000 portfolio and four percent for the other portfolio.

Losing as much as $5,000 in a $25,000 portfolio would be completely devastating. It would take a fifth of your savings. On the other hand, in a $250,000 portfolio, a $5,000 loss is only a two percent loss. While this may be a simple example, it highlights the importance of knowing your risk. This is also what makes position sizing important.

Levels of risk, from lowest to highest, are conservative, moderately conservative, moderately aggressive, aggressive, and very aggressive. This is by no means a scientific scale, but it does give you a guideline that you can follow when you are picking investments.

Determining Risk

With all of the different investment types out there, how can an investor figure how their risk they are able to handle? Everybody is different, and it is pretty hard to come up with an exact model that works for everybody, but there are two things that you need to consider when you are deciding on how much risk you are willing to take.

First is the time horizon. Before you make your actual investment, you must figure out how much time you have to let your money stay invested. If you are going to invest $20,000 today but you need to have a down payment for a new house in a year, investing your money in high-risk stocks isn't the best choice. The riskier your investment is, the bigger its volatility will be. If you have a short time horizon, you may have to sell the securities and take a big loss. When you have a longer time for an investment, it gives you a long time to recoup any losses that you may incur, which makes you, theoretically, more tolerant to higher risks. The means if you are planning on growing that $20,000 for a lakeside cottage that you are going to buy in ten years' time, you could choose to invest in higher-risk stocks.

Second is your bankroll. Figuring out how much money you can lose is the next thing you need to consider when it comes to figuring out your risk tolerance. While this may not be that optimistic, it is the most realistic. When you invest only the money that you can afford to lose, you won't be as pressured to sell the investments due to liquidity or panic. The more money that you have, the greater risk you can take. For example, a person with a $50,000 net worth and another with a $5 million net worth both invests $25,000; the person with the smaller net worth is going to be hit harder by a decline than the other person would.

Once you have looked that these two factors, you can use the risk pyramid approach to balance all of your assets. You can view the pyramid as an asset allocation tool that investors are able to use to diversify their investments according to what their risk profile is. There are three tiers to the pyramid.

1. The foundation of the pyramid is the strongest portion, which helps to support everything that is above it. You should make sure that this consists of low-risk investments and have good returns. This is the biggest area and is made up of the bulk of your assets.

2. The middle section should be made up of investments that are a medium risk and offer a stable return, and it still allows for capital appreciation. While they may be riskier than the assets in the base, these should still be fairly safe.

3. Then the top part is reserved for high-risk investments and should take up the smallest part of your pyramid. It

should be made up of money you are able to lose without facing any serious repercussions. Also, the money that is in the top part needs to be disposable so that you don't end up selling prematurely when capital losses occur.

Position Sizing

Position sizing is the idea that you add the right amount of money to your investments when it comes to your total portfolio size. This tends to be a tough concept to grasp because you have to start thinking about things that a lot of people don't want to think about. That is, how much are you willing to lose on one investment?

A good number to follow is to not risk any more than four of five percent of your portfolio on one idea. If you risk four percent of a $25,000 portfolio, you will limit your possible loss to just $1,000 on your investment.

Trailing Stop

Trailing stop is one way to limit your losses. One common strategy is to follow the 25% rule. This means that you sell if your investment starts to drop 25% from its highs.

If you take the $25,000 portfolio, for example, you would be willing to lose $1,000 on each of your investments, and you decide to use a 25% trailing stop, how much money do you need to invest in your positions? You would invest $4,000. If that

49

$4,000 falls 25%, then you will have lost $1,000. That is a lot less devastating than the example I gave earlier of a 20% loss.

Bonds, Stocks, Cash, and Real Estate

Once you know your risk, you need to make sure that your portfolio has the right mix of bonds, stocks, cash, and real estate. There are many different rules of thought on portfolio diversity. One rule of thumb states that you need to "own your age" in bonds. That would mean that a 30-year-old needs to have 30% of their portfolio made up of bonds, and the rest would be made up of stocks. There is a riskier version of this rule that says you need to have 110 or 120 minus your age in stocks. That would mean the 30-year-old would need to have 80 to 90 percent of their portfolio made up in stocks, and then they would slowly switch over to bonds as they get older.

These types of rules are based upon the idea that a young investor typically has a better chance to recover from any losses that the stock market takes, and so they are able to take advantage of higher returns that equities provide. There are "target-date" mutual funds that provide you with a premixed portfolio of bonds and stocks that will change up as you age.

While these age or time-based rules can be very helpful to get you started out, but these rules are no match for careful financial planning. Since we are talking about stocks and bonds right now, we will continue with them. We'll talk about cash and real estate later.

The best way to figure out your stock and bond allocation in your portfolio is to figure out your risk tolerance, and likely we have already talked about how to figure that out. So, are you risk-averse, moderate, or risk-loving? Your asset allocation is also going to depend on your market portfolio's importance. For example, people often view their IRA or 401k as very important parts of their retirement plan since they will take up the biggest part of their portfolio.

Meanwhile, you can have a different portfolio in an after-tax account that contains punt stocks and is smaller. If your online trading account were to get destroyed, you would still be able to survive. If you end up killing your 401k, you may find that you have to delay your retirement.

There are five different recommended asset allocation models that you can choose from or come up with your own. First up is the conventional asset model. The main recommendation is for you to subtract your age from 100 so that you know how much of your portfolio should be made up of stocks. The idea of this is that as you age, you become more risk-averse since you don't have the same ability to generate income. Starting at age 30, 70% would be stocks and 30% bonds. Then, every five years, the stock percentage decreases by five percent, while the number of the bond increases by five percent.

The next model is the new life asset allocation model. This is where you subtract your age from 120 to figure out the percentages. Studies have found that we are living longer because of scientific advancements and better awareness about our diets. Since stocks tend to do better than bonds over the longer run, we need to have more stocks in our portfolio so that we can take care of our longer lives. The increase and decrease by five percent remains the same, but you will start out at 90% stocks and 10% bonds at the age of 30.

Then you have the survival asset, allocation model. This is great for people who are risk-averse. Here you have a 50/50 allocation, and it increases your chances that your portfolio will outperform when there is a stock market collapse since the bands will increase in value. Bonds are also able to rise when stocks rise.

Then next is the nothing-to-lose asset allocation model. Since stocks tend to outperform bonds, this model is great for people who want to go all-in when it comes to stocks. If your time horizon is long enough, this might be a good idea. Up until the age of 50, all of your assets will be in stocks. Then at age 50 to 60, it will be 90/10. From 60 to 70, the allocations would be 80/20, and then they move to 70/30 and stay there.

For the financial samurai asset allocation model, you will combine the new life model and the nothing to lose model. While stocks will continue to outperform bonds, there will still be volatility. This will help you to prepare for any changes in returns for your stocks and bonds. This is good for people who have several income streams and those who won't depend on their portfolio in retirement. You will begin with 100% in stocks, and then from 35 to 50, your breakdown will be 80/20. From 50 to 65, you will have 70/30. From 65 to 75, you will have 60/40. From 75 on, you will have a breakdown of 50/50.

The one you choose will all depend on what your risk tolerance is. Ideally, you will want your asset allocation to be something that will allow you to sleep well each night and wake up every morning, excited.

Now, as far as cash and real estate go, it works like stocks and bonds, and it all depends on your goals and risk. Some people prefer to be invested more in real estate because it tends to be more stable than the stock market. Like with the stocks and bonds, you can change these percentages as you age, and you probably will want to.

Also, you don't have to have all four of these to make up your net worth. If you don't want to deal with real estate, you don't have to, but it is a good idea to think about. Real estate is definitely touched to beat with comes to stability and long-term returns.

Stocks and bonds can give you back nothing in return, but homes don't typically end up being considered zero in value.

Real estate is also capable of having volatility and risk, so that always has to be considered. If you decided to have a few B class rentals in a decent neighborhood, you could be faced with similar volatility to a bond fund. If you decided to buy a rental in Silicon Valley or have an AirBnB in Vegas solely for its appreciation, they can be a lot riskier, which would be similar to investing in a tech stock.

The main point to this is, you want to have a diversified portfolio, but you also want to make sure that it stays in line with your goals and your risk. You should never invest in anything just because somebody says you should. You should only decide to invest your hard-earned money into things you believe in and that you trust.

Chapter 6:ETF Explained

An ETF or exchange-traded fund is basically a basket of securities like commodities, bonds, stocks, or even a combination of these that you can purchase and sell through a broker. These get put together into one entity that will then offer shares to investors that are traded on the main stock exchange. Every share gives the owner one share in total assets of the ETF. ETFs can give you the best attributes of two of the most popular assets: They mimic how easy stocks are traded, plus they have the diversification of mutual funds.

These have become one of the most valuable and important products that were created for investors recently. They give you many benefits, and if you use them wisely, they are a great way to achieve your investment goals.

ETFs are offered on every asset class from alternative assets such as currencies or commodities to traditional investments. The structure of an ETF lets investors stay away from short-term capital gains taxes, to gain leverage and too short markets.

After a few false starts, ETFs started in 1993 with a product known by the symbol SPY or as traders call them "spiders," which became the biggest volume ETF in history. There are about one trillion dollars that have been invested in ETFs and almost 1,000 ETF products that get traded on the stock exchange.

These funds have taken the world by storm, and investors have taken advantage of all the opportunities they give to you. Investors have put around $3.5 trillion into ETFs. There are hundreds if not thousands of various ETFs available to buy.

How popular ETFs have become is because of their unique features and characteristics. I will get more into the details below. ETFs have opened the door to various investments that most investors hadn't ever had access to before. Because of the broad focus, simplicity, diversification, and efficiency, ETFs offer you benefits that no other investment could match.

ETFs normally track different benchmarks. Every fund will invest with the objective of matching returns that the fund chose. There are some ETFs that have managers that seek out their own investments, but since the disclosure rules require these funds to let the investors know about their holdings daily. Most managers who like to manage money using strategies will choose other tools rather than ETFs.

Most ETFs are registered by investment companies for tax reasons. This means that they normally don't pay corporate taxes a the fund level. Any taxable income they give you has to be passed to their shareholders. Anybody who has invested in ETFs are entitled to get their proportional share that the ETF generates. Funds normally accumulate some dividends in a short amount of time, and then they distribute the total either monthly, quarterly, or annually.

One great aspect of the ETF is the way shares get made and redeemed. Instead of working with shareholders, most ETFs will use special markets to make the trades. These markets create new shares by buying the stocks or investments held by the fund and deliver them to the company, which will issue shares that the market can then sell. The market can deliver a huge block of ETF shares to the company and get securities back. This structure makes sure that the market for ETFs stays effective, and it contributes to some tax advantages.

The fund provider will own the assets. They design funds to track performances of stocks and then will sell their shares to investors. The shareholders will own a part of the ETF, but they don't actually own the assets in the fund. ETF investors that track the stock market will be given dividend payments, or they will reinvest.

Even though ETFs have been created to track the value of the asset, whether it is a basket of stocks or a commodity such as gold, they will trade at prices that the market determines that are usually different from the asset. Since there are things like expenses, longer-term returns are going to vary from those of the assets.

Stocks Vs. Mutual Funds Vs. ETFs

ETFs will have fewer fees than mutual funds. This is why they are so popular. The normal US equity mutual fund will charge 1.42 percent in yearly expenses. This is called an expense ratio. An ETF average fee is about 0.53 percent.

ETFs do offer tax advantages for their investors. There is normally more turnover with mutual funds as related to an ETF. Selling and purchasing can bring in capital gains. If an investor sells a mutual fund, the manager has to get the cash through selling securities. This is also able to provide capital gains. In both of these scenarios, investors will have to pay these taxes.

ETFs are very popular, but how many mutual funds available is still going to be higher. These two also have different management structures.

Just like stocks, you can trade ETFs on exchanges, and they are provided with their own symbols on the ticker that allows you to track what they are doing. This is where their similarities stop since ETFs are a group of assets, where a stock is representative of a single company.

Closed-end Funds Vs. ETFs

Closed-end funds are as well known as ETFs or mutual funds. This small market mixes together some of the attributes of ETFs and mutual funds. They have a similar structure to mutual funds, and they have been around longer than ETFs. They make a trade on the stock exchanges, and this gives you the same advantages of trading that ETFs give you.

The largest difference between these two is the amount of outstanding shares. ETFs have mechanisms where market participants can redeem or create a large block of ETF shares with the broker that manages the ETF. Because of this, if there is a high demand for a specific share, these participants can go to the manager and purchase some shares that they can sell to other investors on the exchange.

In contrast, there are just a certain number of shared that will be available at any given time. Whatever the company manages, the closed-end fund isn't able to issue new shares whenever they want to. They have to go through the same procedures as when they are trading any other stock on the market.

Since these companies don't like doing that, the supply and demand with investors looking for a fund play huge roles in pricing closed-end shares. If everybody is interested in a certain fund, then they might trade at well above what the normal value of that fund's assets suggests is the right number. If a fund loses its favor, then its shares can be traded cheaper than the actual value that is held within the fund. Since investors can't demand for a fund to turn over its underlying investment, these discounts might last for several years.

Closed-end funds aren't favored anymore since they have to be actively managed and have fees that are extremely high. There are some areas within the market where these closed-end funds still prosper. Investors in ETFs can normally find a better deal by looking for ETFs that have the same objectives.

Cons and Pros of ETFs

Investors have flocked to ETFs due to their access to diversified products, cheapness, and simplicity.

Pros

- Tax benefits: Investors get taxed only if they sell the investment, but mutual funds incur taxes over the life of your investment.

- Transparency: Anybody who has access to the internet can look for an ETF's price. The holding is open to the public. Mutual funds only get disclosed quarterly or monthly.

- Diversification: It is easy to think about diversification when talking about broad market verticals. For example, commodities, bonds, or stocks allow investors to diversify across horizontals such as industries. It takes effort and money to purchase all the components in one basket. With one click of your mouse, an ETF can bring your portfolio these benefits.

Cons

- Risk of the ETF closing: The main reason that this could happen is if a fund has not brought in enough money to cover the cost of administration. The largest inconvenience that a shuttered ETF is investors must sell faster than they would regularly want to, and it could cause a loss. You are also faced with having to reinvest and also the problem of taxes.

- Finding buyers for the ETF: Just like with all securities, you are going to be at the market's mercy when you want to sell. Any ETF that isn't traded a lot is going to be harder to sell.

- Trading costs: The cost of an ETF might not end after you pay the expense ratio. You could be faced with commission fees from brokers since ETFs are exchange-traded. There are some brokers who have dropped their commissions for ETFs, but not all of them have done so.

How to Shop for ETFs

You need to know that, while costs for ETFs are normally lower, they tend to vary depending on the funds. It all depends on who issues it and its demand and complexity. The biggest brokers are Vanguard, SPDR, and iShares. ETFs that track on the same index are going to come at different costs.

A trend for shoppers has been that some brokerages have dropped their commissions to zero.

Most ETFs get managed passively. They just track an index. There some who prefer a hands-on approach that mutual funds give. These get run by professional managers. Their goal is to outperform the market. Some ETFs get actively managed and tend to mimic mutual funds, but these will often have a lot of high fees. You need to think about how you want to invest before you decide to buy it. Just because you can get an ETF cheap does not mean that is will fit into your portfolio.

How to Invest

There are many ways you can invest in ETFs; it basically comes down to your personal preference. For investors who like to be hands-on, the ETF world is only a couple of clicks away. There are all part of stander broker offerings, although how many they offer will change from broker to broker. Robo-advisors will build their portfolio out of ETFs, and this gives investors access to their assets.

ETFs have nuances that you need to understand. As long as you know the basics, you can choose if an ETF makes sense in your portfolio. What is stopping you from starting your journey of investing in ETFs?

Types of ETFs

- Alternative Investment ETFs: ETFs let investors trade volatility or get exposure to certain investment strategies like covered call writing or currency carry.

- Exchange-traded notes: Basically, debt securities that are backed by a creditworthy bank that was created to give access to liquid markets, and they have added in the benefit of generating no capital gains taxes.

- Actively managed ETFs: These were created to outperform an index. This is different from most ETFs that were created to track an index.

- Inverse ETFs: These were designed to profit if there is a decline in the index or market.

- Foreign market ETFs: These were designed to track markets that aren't in the United States like Hong Kong's Hang Seng or Japan's Nikkei Index.

- Style ETFs: These were designed to track market capitalization focus or investment style like small-cap growth or large-cap value.

- Commodity ETFs: These were designed to track a commodity's price like corn, oil, or gold.

- Industry and Sector ETFs: These were designed to give exposure to a certain industry like high technology, pharmaceuticals, or oil.

- Bond ETFs: These were designed to give exposure to every type of bond that is available like high-yield, international, municipal, corporate, U.S. Treasury, and many more.

- Market ETFs: These were designed to track on a certain index such as NASDAQ or S&P 500.

Disadvantages

Even though they are superior in many aspects, ETFs do have some drawbacks:

- Settlement dates: Sales of ETFs don't get settled for two days after the transaction. This means that when you sell one, the funds from that sale won't be available for you to reinvest for two days.

- Tracking error: Normally, ETFs track the index fairly well, but technical problems could cause some discrepancies.

- Illiquidity: Some ETFs that are thinly traded will have wide spreads, and this means that you will be purchasing on the high end of the spread and selling on the low end.

- Trading costs: If you frequently invest small amounts, there might be alternatives that cost less if you buy then straight from the company as a no-load fund.

Advantages

- Trading transactions: Since these get traded just like stocks, you can put in many types of orders that you can't do with mutual funds.

- Tax-efficient: You have more control over when you pay your capital gains tax.

- Lower fees: There isn't any sales load, but brokerage commissions will apply.

- Sell and buy at any time during the day: In contrast, mutual funds only settle at the close of the market.

The hallmark of the ETF industry has always been innovations since it started about 25 years ago. There will be more ETFs that get introduced in the future. Even though innovation is an investors' net, it is important that you realize that all ETFs don't get created equal. You have to do lots of research before you decide to invest in an ETF. You need to make sure you consider all the factors to make sure that the ETF is the best way for you to reach your investment goals.

Chapter 7: Accumulation Plan for Life in ETF

A simple definition of an accumulation plan is a financial strategy where investors try to build the value of their portfolio. When talking about mutual funds, this becomes a formal arrangement where investors contribute a certain amount of money into the fund periodically. By doing this, they are accumulating a larger investment in the fund through the increase of the value of the fund and their contributions.

Breaking It Down

In accounting and economics, capital accumulation is usually equal to the investment of savings or income, especially when dealing with capital goods. Capital accumulation refers to:

- Investing in nonproductive physical assets like works of art or residential real estate that might increase in value.

- Investing in assets represented on paper, capital gains, fees, royalties, rent, interest, or yielding profit.

- Investing in tangible means of production like development, research, and acquisitions that could increase your capital flow.

Why Do You Need An Accumulation Plan?

Having a good accumulation plan is necessary if you want to create a financial nest egg for your retirement. Most investors will do this by reinvesting in capital gains and dividends and with regular contributions. Basically, the main goal is to keep your funds invested, reinvest capital gains and income, and let these compounds for as long as you can.

Accumulation plans could be useful for investors who want to build a position in mutual funds over an amount of time. It can also give you the benefits of "dollar-cost averaging."

Voluntary Plan

This is a way of investing where an investor periodically invests small amounts of money into a mutual fund, which will create a large position for you over a period of time.

When you spread these contributions over an amount of time, you will reap the benefits of "dollar-cost averaging" since the contributions are going to purchase more shares of a specific fund when the price is low rather than when it is high. This is a great solution for anybody who wants to create a portfolio but isn't can't afford to invest huge amounts at one time.

In addition to having the advantage of building an investment over an amount of time, this plan gives you the benefit of investing in mutual funds that are very low risk. This plan also lets investors take advantage of "dollar-cost averaging."

Hire a Professional

It isn't that hard to find a financial advisor that will fit your needs. A quick search on Google and you should be able to find a list of advisors in your area. Now, you might have to put in some research to find the best ones or the ones you can afford. Once you find your advisor, they can help you reach your financial goals.

Investing in ETFs

ETFs have become very popular, and they could play a huge role in your investment strategy. Investors have put over $5 trillion into ETFs. The last trillion didn't even take one year to accumulate.

This is why ETFs offer many advantages for investors, and they can be part of your investment strategy. It doesn't matter how complex or basic your strategy is.

ETFs are great for investors who are just starting out since they give you many benefits like low investment threshold, diversification, large investment choices, abundant liquidity, and low expense ratios.

These features make ETFs perfect for various investment and trading strategies that are used by new investors and traders. Here are the best strategies for anyone who wants to invest in ETFs.

- Dollar-Cost Averaging

We will start with the most basic strategy, which is dollar-cost averaging. Dollar-cost averaging is a technique of purchasing a specific dollar amount of an asset on a regular basis. It doesn't matter how much the cost of the asset changes. Investors who are just starting out are normally young people who have worked for some time and have a stable income. They make enough to be able to save a bit of money every month. These investors should be able to take a couple hundred each month, and rather than putting it into a savings account, they could invest it into an ETF or many ETFs.

There are some advantages to this type of investing for beginners. The first one is that it creates discipline to help you save. Most financial planners will tell you that you have to pay yourself first. This is what you get when you save regularly. The second one is when you invest the same amount of money in an ETF each month; you are going to accumulate more when the price of an ETF is low and less when the price of an ETF is high. This will average out how much you spend on your holdings. With time, this approach could pay off very well if you remain disciplined.

- Asset Allocation

This basically means that you allocate a part of your portfolio to different asset categories like cash, commodities, bonds, and stocks so you can diversify. This is a very powerful investing tool. Since most ETFs have a low investment threshold, it makes it easy for beginners to implement an asset allocation strategy. It all depends on your risk tolerance and investment time horizon. Young investors might be completely invested in their ETFs during their 20s since their high-risk tolerance and investment time horizons are higher. As they get into their 30s and start making lifestyle changes like buying a house, starting a family, they might change to a less aggressive mix like 40 percent in bond ETFs and 60 percent in equity ETFs.

- Swing Trading

These are trades that like taking advantage of large swings in commodities, currencies, or stocks. These could take anywhere from a couple of weeks to a couple of days to get them worked out. This isn't like day trades that are never left open overnight.

What makes ETFs suitable for swing trading are their tight bid spreads and diversification. Since ETFs are available for a wide range of sectors and various investment classes, any beginner could choose to trade their ETFs that are based on an asset class or sector where they have some knowledge or expertise. Somebody who has a background in technology might have a bit of advantage when trading technical ETFs. A beginning trader who tracks the markets might prefer to trade some of the commodity ETFs that are available. Since ETFs are normally baskets of assets and stocks, they might not show the same price movements as just one stock in a bull market. Because of their diversification, this makes them not as susceptible to large downward moves. This gives you some protection against erosion.

- Sector Rotation

ETFs make it easy for beginners to use sector rotation based on different stages of the economic cycle.

Let's say an investor has been investing in the biotechnology sector. With this stock up 137 percent over the past five years, this investor might want to take the profits from this ETF and put it into a different sector like consumer staples.

- Short Selling

This is a sale of a financial instrument or borrowed security. It is normally a risky endeavor for investors and shouldn't ever be attempted by beginners. Short selling an ETF is better for shorting single stocks since it has a lower risk of a short squeeze. A short squeeze is a trading secret where a commodity or security that was heavily shorted all of a sudden starts to spike higher.

Using ETFs to short sell helps a trader take advantage of broad investment themes. If a more advanced beginner is familiar with the risks of shorting, but they want to initiate a short position in the emerging market. Please note that beginners should stay away from double or triple-leveraged inverse ETFs that try to find results that are equal to two or three times the inverse of a one-day price change.

- Seasonal Trends

Another tool to help beginners capitalize on seasonal trends are ETFs. There are two seasonal trends that are very popular. One is known as the "sell in May and go away." This is referring to the fact that equities in the US normally underperform during the six month period from May until October as compared to the November to April time frame. The other trend is that gold will gain during the months of September to October. This is due to strong demands from India before the Diwali festival of lights and wedding season that normally falls between the middle of October to the middle of November. You could exploit the market's weakness by shorting the SPDR S&P 500 ETF near the end of April or the first of May or closing the short position at the end of October just after the market swoons. Any beginner could take advantage of the strength of gold by purchasing units in a gold ETF during late summer and then closing out after several months. Please note that seasonal trends don't happen as you think they will. Stop losses are normally recommended for trading positions to cap the large losses.

- Hedging

A beginning trader might need to protect or hedge against a downside risk if they have a large portfolio, maybe one that was acquired because of an inheritance. Let's say you inherited a large portfolio of blue chips and are worried about the risk of a huge decline inequities. One solution would be to purchase put options. Because most beginners aren't familiar with trading strategies, one alternate strategy is initiating a short position in broad market ETFs. If the market goes down as expected, your equity position gets hedged effectively because declines in your portfolio get offset by gains in the short position. Please note that your gains could be capped if the market goes up because gains get offset by losses in short ETF position. Basically, ETFs give beginners an effective and easy way of hedging.

Reinvesting Dividends from ETFs

A great way to grow your portfolio without having to get out your wallet is to reinvest the dividends that you earn from your investments. Even though mutual funds make dividend reinvestment easy, reinvesting those dividends can become complicated. You can make the reinvestments manual by buying more shares with the money you have earned, or you can do it automatically.

Not every ETF comes with an automatic reinvestment program. The longer the settlement time an ETF has, along with their trading, could make reinvesting ineffective

- Dividend Reinvestment Plans or DRIP

This is simply a program that is offered by brokerage firms, ETFs, or mutual funds that let investors automatically use their dividends to buy more shares of a security. Most people do this with mutual funds, but it can also be done with ETFs.

Even though DRIPs provide you with a handier and more convenient way to increase your investment, they can end up creating problems. Some firms will let you use DRIP buy only if you buy a complete share. If there is any money left over, it will be added to your investor's account that you could forget about. Other firms will pool your dividends and then only reinvest them on a monthly or quarterly basis.

There are some who will reinvest as soon as the market opens up on payday, while others will wait until after the case has been deposited. This is normally later during the day. Since ETFs get traded like stocks, and their prices vary throughout the day, reinvesting at the beginning of the day might purchase a different number of shares that the trade that waited until later. This is just one drawback of automatically reinvesting your ETF dividends. You lose control of your trade and can't "time" the market to make it advantageous.

- Manual Reinvestment

If you don't have a DRIP option, or if your ETFs don't allow automatic reinvestments, you can reinvest your dividends manually. This basically means you take the cash you have earned and execute another trade to purchase more ETF shares. This will depend on where you have your investment account. You could have to pay a commission. Some brokerage firms have commission-free dividend reinvestments.

Even though manual investing isn't as convenient as DRIP, it does give the investor more control. Instead of just paying the market price for a new share, you can choose to wait if you think the price might drop. It also gives you the option of holding your dividends in cash if you think the ETF isn't performing the way you want it to, and you would like to invest someplace else.

If you do end up manually reinvesting, make sure you know how the settlement will delay your buying power. It can take payments longer to settle since ETFs rely on brokerages to track shareholders. ETF payments tend to take three or more days to settle. If the ETF is doing good, this long wait time could cause you to have to pay more for another share.

Reinvesting is an easy way to help your portfolio increase. Due to some of the practices with ETFs, they can be a bit more difficult to reinvest than mutual funds. Speak with your firm to see if you have a DRIP option. If you have to reinvest manually, keep track of the time to make sure you don't time the reinvestment poorly. Creating an order during the same time that the dividend is deposited may not provide you with the best price. You can use manual reinvestments to your advantage by actively managing your trades.

Chapter 8: The Best ETF

Mutual funds and retirement investing go hand in hand. Why shouldn't they? Mutual funds predate ETFs by more than 60 years. Most of the 401k plans don't hold anything but mutual funds. This is why most people link them together.

Don't look over ETFs. Most of the ETFs out there are great trading vehicles and tactical strategies. Some are extremely cheap that can give you what you need for retirement, which is income, protection, and diversification.

ETFs are very popular for anyone who wants to grow their money with long- and short-term horizons. ETFs, let you sell and purchase funds such as stock on the stock exchange. This is different than the normal mutual funds that just let you trade at the end of the business day. ETFs have a combination of quick liquidity and instant diversification. This is the best reason to think about them first when wanting to invest for the first time or as a part of your portfolio.

Most of the ETFs are just simple index funds. They will track just like bonds, stocks, or other investments. This is an inexpensive strategy since you won't be paying a manager to select and analyze your stocks. The good news is that it works.

If you like the strategy of buying and holding and allowing carefully researched investments accumulate returns with time,

ETFs just might be the right choice for you. Warren Buffett knows that it is hard to beat index funds. This is why he has place 90 percent of his money that he is bequeathing to his wife and is invested in an S&P 500 ETF.

You don't need to be like Buffett and put all your cash into one of these funds. But these are a low-cost and attractive choice for small and large investors.

ETFs trade almost instantly if you enter a trade with your broker or online. Most ETFs will track just like any stock on the Dow Jones or S&P 500. ETFs can focus on anything that a normal fund can.

Just like any investment, ETFs do have risks. Normally a riskier investment will lead to larger returns. ETFs will follow this same pattern. Funds that focus on bonds and broad, diverse market funds normally offer the lowest risks. Narrower funds and commodity options normally bring more volatility and risk.

The decisions you make about your investments need to align with your financial goals. You need to know your risk tolerance. You have to know if you can afford to lose all or some of your investments and how the choices you make will fit into your financial plan.

You need to think about the underlying assets before you purchase an ETF, you aren't directly purchasing a company's bonds or stock. Rather, you are placing money into a fund that will then buy a "basket" of bonds and stocks for you. Be sure that the fund you are purchasing will invest in assets that you ultimately would choose for yourself.

You need to take into account the volatility and risks. Some people are fine taking risks and betting that these will pay off with large returns. Others want to stay away from large ups and downs. They are more concerned with making sure they have a steady income and preserving their capital. You will need to pick an ETF that will line up with your tolerance for risks.

Watch out for fees. There are some ETFs that are completely free of fees. These ETFs are a brand new concept. Before that, getting a competitive ETF from a company like Schwab, Fidelity, and Vanguard was on top of the competition, with fees as low as .1 percent. The most expensive ETF charged 9.2 percent. You need to compare all the ETFs you are interested in for hidden fees and specific features before you decide to purchase them.

You shouldn't ever purchase an investment if you don't totally know all the risks. If you any concerns, you need to consult with an expert or financial advisor before you enter your trade order.

Here are the best ETFs on the market today:

- "Vanguard S&P 500"

This is the best ETF, and it comes from that biggest mutual fund company. This ETF will track the S&P 500. Its expense ratio is only 0.04 percent. Warren Buffet has recommended this company by name.

Purchasing one of these funds will give you a piece of the 500 largest companies in the US. This gives you a lot of diversity along with a safety net since every investment is focused on the United States.

The S&P 500 is a proxy for the entire economy of the US. It brings a return of about ten percent each year. Even though the past performance isn't a guarantee of how the market will perform in the future as it could go down at any moment. This ETF would be a great choice.

- "Invesco QQQ Trust"

This company only owns Nasdaq stocks that aren't financial. This makes it a tech-heavy fund with some names that you are familiar with. Their ETF is the biggest one around and it is very liquid. It isn't expensive either. It only costs $20 per year for every $10,000 you have invested. It did have a bad performance during 2018. This just shows you how broad the market really is.

This isn't saying anything negative about the ETF since it was up almost 33 percent the year before.

- "Fidelity ZERO Total Market Index Fund"

This ETF doesn't have much of a history; it doesn't have any minimums or fees. If you would like to invest for free, this is a great option. There isn't a minimum to invest. This makes it an option for new investors and people who need retirement accounts. The index will focus on the complete return based on the stock market in the US. This makes it more diversified than any S&P 500 fund.

This ETF offers an almost identical performance to the Dow Jones index. In the last ten years, it has outperformed large blends.

- "iShares Core S&P 500"

This ETF tracks the S&P 500. This gives it a broad-based, diversified portfolio in the largest company in America. This fund is backed by the company, Blackrock. The ETF is the biggest around. It has $160 billion in assets. This fund was created in 2000. It has an annual cost of only $4 for each $10,000 that you invest. The bad performance during 2018 shows the market's performance of -4.4%.

- "SPDF S&P 500"

You read that right S&P 500 does have more than one spot on the list. While the VOO from Vanguard is a great idea for long-term investors, this one is the most traded ETF out there.

Since this will track the S&P 500, active investors can use this to sell and purchase stocks in one trade. This launched back in 1993 as the very first ETF. Traders prefer this ETF because it is very liquid. It does charge a 0.095 percent ratio that is higher than Vanguard's. Because it is so popular and is traded frequently, most investors are happy to spend some money on this ETF.

- "ProShares VIX Short-Term Futures"

This is an unusual ETF since it lets investors profit on the market's volatility instead of a certain security. If the volatility goes higher, this ETF will increase in value. It is a great short-term trade since it needs to roll derivatives regularly. This can cost the ETF money with time. In spite of having only a few assets, the fund is liquid. Its expense ratio costs $87 each year for every $10,000 you invest.

- "iShares Russell 2000"

This tracks2,000 small stocks. It is comprised of the littlest 2,000 on the Russell 3000 index. This is a great way to track the stock market, but it focuses on the small companies within the public market rather than the largest.

This has an expense ratio of 0.19 percent. This is lower than most mutual funds but nowhere close to the bottom of the ETFs. If you compare it to any S&P 500 fund, iShare Russell 2000 managers will have four times the number of stocks to purchase and sell to keep the fund with the index.

There are a few investors who argue that small stocks have the room to grow more than the larger stocks, while others will argue that small stocks are more volatile and risky. If you want to purchase a huge batch of companies with one purchase, this is the best way to go.

- "Vanguard High Dividend Yield"

This ETF will track the "FTSE High Dividend Yield Index." This index includes American stocks that pay high yields. It has about $23 billion dollars to manage, and this makes it very liquid. It is sponsored by Vanguard, the most reputable name in the business. This ETF was created in 2006. It only charges $6 for each $10,000 that you have invested. It won't cut into the payout too much.

- "Schwab U.S. Dividend Equity"

Schwab brings us another low-cost ETF. This ETF is a great choice if you want to turn your portfolio into cash. This fund will focus on large companies that have stable dividends. Retirees who are looking to earn money from their portfolio without having to sell their stocks will use dividend stocks as an investment. This ETF is managed to track on the Dow Jones. It charges a competitive 0.07 percent expense ratio.

- "Vanguard Health Care Index Fund"

Another Vanguard fund makes an appearance. This fund charges ten dollars for each $10,000 that you have invested. This allows you to be exposed to more than 300 stocks on the sector. This can protect you from any negative performances in the industry. If a radical change affects healthcare in general, this fund stays protected. This fund was created in 2004 and has about $9.4 billion in assets.

- "SPDR Gold Trust"

If you would like to invest in gold without having to actually buy a bar of gold, this would be your best option. It charges 0.04 percent for its expense ratio. Gold is normally used a hedge fund against a decline in the market. If the economy or stocks fall, investors normally turn to gold as a safety net. This means that gold will usually trade inversely to the more popular index. Just remember that if you want to turn some of your hard-earned money into gold.

- "Vanguard FTSE Developed Markets"

If you want to add some international flair to your portfolio, companies in well-developed countries usually offer a good balance of return and risk. Funds that are as well developed might be more tempting, but be careful because these are riskier than the developed markets.

This ETF follows the "FTSE Developed All Cap ex US Index." This means that it will follow companies of any size in any developed country other than the US. This puts stocks in the developed Pacific nations, Europe, and Canada into your portfolio easily. It only charges an expense ratio of 0.07 percent.

- "iShares MSCI EAFE"

You have to make sure your portfolio is diversified because there isn't any investment that will work all the time. This ETF holds more than 900 stocks from over 12 countries, including France, the United Kingdom, and Japan. Even though it is a blended fund, most of these caps will yield a lot more than their American counterparts. This can lead to more money than the S&P 500.

- "Vanguard Total Stock Market"

If you aren't sure which index you should follow, or you want to invest in various market capitalization and sectors, this might be for you. This ETF covers the whole domestic stock market. This is a balanced fund that has a great mix of blue-chip, midcap, and small-cap stocks. This has a low expense ratio of 0.03 percent.

- "iShares Cohen & Steers REIT"

This is a real estate investment trust. They are a bit different than normal stocks. These were created by Congress back in the 60s to give investors access to real estate. It would be very hard for normal people to find a million dollars to buy or lease a strip mall or office building. Any investor can find a few hundred dollars for a couple of shares.

These are great for retirement investors for several reasons. These funds are obligated to pay out no less than 9 percent of their profits to their shareholders. This makes real estate a great source of income for retired people.

This ETF combines the expertise of Cohen and Steers with iShares to create a fund that protects you from market crashes. This ETF gives less than other REITs. It does have an emphasis on high quality and gives better price-performance. This makes it a winner.

- "Vanguard Total World Stock"

This is the best ETF for an investor who wants a whole world of stock without purchasing numerous funds. It might just be the only stock that you will ever need. It places over 8,000 stocks within your reach from all over the world. It has a yield of about 2.3 percent and only costs 0.9 percent. This is truly a one-stop-shop for equities. It is very cheap for everything you get. At this moment, it yields more than the US markets.

- "SPDR Bloomberg Barclays 1-3 Month T-Bill"

This is a money market ETF and is designed to protect you and your assets while you are earning money. These invest in short-term, high-quality debt like Treasury notes or CDs. They won't yield much, but they are a very low risk. This makes them ideal during turbulent markets.

There are other money markets ETFs, but this one is an inexpensive and solid choice. You can't find many small ETFs out there. This one only holds 15 very short-term Treasury issues that range from one to three months. It has an average duration of only 29 days.

- "Vanguard Total Bond Market"

There is a place in most portfolios for bonds, especially retirement accounts. This is because they give out fixed distributions that retired people can use as income. It can help if you have other uncorrelated assets. Why are bond funds better than individual bonds? They are harder to research than other stocks. They normally don't get covered by the media. Bond funds take the responsibility off your place, and you get a bonus of spreading the risk across hundreds and possibly thousands of bonds. This has an expense ratio of 0.035 percent.

Chapter 9: Live On Income With Dividends in ETF, or Sell Everything and Make The Good Life

You might still be a bit confused as to how you make money from ETFs. Contrary to popular belief, ETFs aren't magic or lottery tickets. Just like most things, they do have their cons and pros that need to be weighed carefully. You have to seriously think about your personal resources, preferences, circumstances, and any other relevant factor. This chapter will give you an understanding of how profits get generated for ETF investors, so hopefully, it will give you some questions to ask your financial advisor or help you make better choices about your portfolio.

How ETFs Make You Money

Getting money from ETFs is just like getting money from investing in mutual funds since they operate just about identically. How you make money on your ETFs all depends on the kind of investment it holds.

An ETF is kind of like a trust fund. It might invest in famous indexes like the S&P 500 or The Dow Jones, preferred stock, commodities like silver or gold, bonds, or stocks. So, what exactly does this mean for an investor? It basically comes down to one thing: The way you make money from your ETF all depends on the underlying investment of said ETF with time.

Basically, this is saying that if you own an ETF that focuses on stocks that pay high dividends, you hope to make money from dividends paid from the same stocks and capital gains.

If you own an ETF known as a bond fund, you are hoping to make money from interest. If you have an ETF in real estate, you are hoping to make money from the income generated by other real estate owned, office buildings, hotels, apartments, capital gains on property sales, and underlying rents.

Mutual Funds and ETFs Make Money Similarly

Just like mutual funds, there are three things that can help you increase the return on your ETF with time. These same things will hold true when you are trying to make money with an ETF:

- Stay Focused on the Long Term

ETFs normally perform in line with their holdings short of some type of structural problem or other events. This basically means that if you hold an ETF, you might have to suffer through some bad highs and lows in the market value during the year. You might see time like during 2007 and 2009 when your holdings are down between 20 and 50 percent or more. If you can't handle dealing with things like this, you don't have any business investing in these types of securities. There aren't any guarantees about what the future is going to look like, but historically, the time has gotten rid of most of that volatility and investors will get rewarded well.

- Keep the Expenses Reasonable

Normally, this isn't a huge problem since ETFs have expenses that are affordable. This is the main reason that investors prefer them over individually managed accounts. Basically, this means that you, a financial advisor, or a financial planner can put together a portfolio of diversified holding and pick up things such as ETFs that will focus on industries or individual sectors for a ration like .50 percent annually.

- If You Don't Understand the ETF, Don't Invest In It

You will find some crazy ETFs out there. Some of these will utilize short stocks and super leverage, some that only invest in countries that are just above the third world, still others that will concentrate in certain industries or sectors. Warren Buffett likes saying that the first rule to making money is not to ever lose any. The next rule is to look at rule number one. You need to know exactly what the underlying holding of every ETF you own so that you know why you invested in it.

The main thing you need to remember is that ETFs are similar to other investments because they won't solve every problem. They are only a tool.

Dividends on ETFs

There are two types of dividends issued on ETFs. These are non-qualifies and qualified dividends.

If you own ETFs, you might receive money in the form of dividends. These could get pain monthly or at other intervals. It all depends on the particular ETF. It's important to know that all dividends aren't treated equally when talking about taxes.

Let's look closer at the types of dividends.

- Nonqualified Dividends

These don't get designated by the ETF as qualifies since they may have been payable on stocks that were held by the ETF for two months or less. These get taxed at regular income rates. Nonqualified dividends are the total dividends less any portion of the total dividend that gets treated as qualified dividends.

- Qualified Dividends

These get designated by the ETF as being qualified. This means that they qualify to get taxed at the same rate as capital gains. It all depends on the investor's taxable income and MAGI or modified adjusted gross income. The dividends get pain on the stock that is held by the ETF. They have to own them for over two months during any 121 day period that starts two months before the ex-dividend date. Plus, the investor has to own shares in the ETF that is paying the dividend for over two months during the same 121-day time frame that starts two months before the ex-dividend date. This basically meant that if you actively trade ETFs, you won't meet these requirements.

Please note that qualified dividends get taxed at the same rats as capital gains, you can't use them to offset capital losses.

Other Distributions

It all depends on the kind of ETF; other distributions might not be qualified dividends. Here are a few examples of other kinds of distributions:

- REIT or real estate investment trust ETFs normally pay nonqualified dividends.

- Fixed-income ETFs will pay you interest and not dividends.

1. NII or Net Investment Income Tax

If you make a lot of money, your dividends might be subject to a Medicare tax of 3.8 percent plus any income tax on the dividends. This tax will apply to the net investment income.

2. Reporting Dividends

Wherever you hold your ETFs has to send a report to the IRS annually, and they will send you any payments on your dividends that were over ten dollars. They will send you Form 1099-DIV.

3. Reinvesting Dividends

You could choose to either use your dividends to purchase more shares within the same ETF. There might be some commissions for reinvesting the dividends. You will need to check with the firm or financial institution that holds your ETFs.

4. Dividends ETFs

The dividend ETF is made up of stocks that pay dividends that you can track on an index. This ETF will pay dividends to all their investors that can be either non-qualified or qualified dividends.

If you get a fairly large amount of dividends from your ETFs, you might need to pay quarterly taxes. You might need to talk with your tax advisor to figure out your tax needs and make sure that you report your dividends on your yearly tax return.

A Guide to ETF Dividends

There are many great reasons to add dividend stocks to your portfolio. Other than the obvious reason for creating money, dividends usually hold up better than their counterparts during the rough times. They aren't as volatile on the market.

Owning dividend stocks won't be right for everybody. Most investors don't have time, desire, or knowledge to research and then construct a portfolio of stocks; if this sounds like you, if you just want to make a solid portfolio before you add individual stocks, purchasing ETFs might be the best way to get some exposure.

- Individual Dividend Stocks Vs. ETFs

There are both drawbacks and benefits to both ETF investing and purchasing individual dividend stocks.

The phrase dividend stock refers to any stock that makes any cash payment to its shareholders regularly. These can be smart choices for investors who are looking for income since they can create a steady income but has more long-term growth than other investments such as bonds. Why would you use ETFs to purchase dividend stocks?

ETFs will simplify the process. ETFs allow you to purchase a portfolio of well-diversified stocks with one investment and without having to research or the risk that comes with purchasing stocks.

One drawback to ETF investing is you are going to pay continuous investment fees. These might be small and possibly negligible sometimes, but portfolio managers never work for free. ETFs charge investors fees that cover expenses.

Individual stocks do have some benefits. The biggest one is individual stocks could beat the index with time, while most of the ETFs are passive investments that will track on an index. Passive ETFs will match the same performance as a stock on the index. A portfolio of individual stock could underperform on a specific index with time. An ETF will guarantees that you will match the index's performance after the fees.

- How Much Does It Cost to Invest in ETFs

I have mentioned the word fee a couple times now, so let's talk about the cost of investing in ETFs. There are two costs you should know: trading commissions and ongoing investment fees.

Expense ratios are a percentage of the assets and get paid out of the assets. You don't get billed directly. If you have an expense ratio of .3 percent meant that for every $2,000 you invested, you are going to pay $6 in annual fees.

Your broker might charge you a trading commission just like you would if you had purchased a stock. These could vary significantly depending on the brokerage you use. Some brokers have an ETF program where certain ETFs are commission-free, but this selection is normally limited and changes a lot.

- Tax Implications

If you purchase your ETFs using your IRA, you don't have to worry about any tax implication regularly. If you invest in a standard brokerage account, there will be some tax implications.

There are capital gains taxes. These are taxes on any profit you get from your ETF shares. Capital gains don't get taxed until you sell the shared. At this point, they are called realized capital gains. If your ETF goes up from $$25 to $500 per share and you haven't sold it, it will still be an unrealized gain and won't be taxable.

When you sell it for a profit, there will be various capital gains tax rates that will apply depending on how long you have owned the shares. If you have owned them for over one year, you will get taxed at long-term capital gains rates. These are normally lower than the corresponding tax brackets for each level of income. If you have owned your share for less than one year, any realized gains are going to be taxed like any ordinary income, according to your tax bracket within the year that you decided to sell the shares.

The other tax issue you have to be aware of is dividend taxes. ETF dividends are taxable in the year that you bought them. Most dividends, meet the IRS definition of qualified dividends that get taxed at the same tax rate as long-term capital gains. There are exceptions. Some international stock ETFs won't qualify for preferential tax treatment.

Your broker will keep track of what dividends need to be classified in whatever manner. They will report that total to you and the IRS on a 1099-DIV at the end of the year.

- Passive Vs. Active ETFs

There are two types of mutual funds and ETFs; one is passively managed funds called index funds. The other one is actively managed funds.

Passively managed index funds will track an index along with the investment. Because you don't need any strategy to invest, index funds have a lower expense ratio.

Actively managed funds won't track a certain index. They will employ investment manages to create a portfolio of commodities, bonds, or stocks with the end goal of beating a certain index. Since they paid their active managers, actively managed funds usually have a high expense ratio.

- Should You Invest in ETFs

A good ETF dividend could be a great fit in any long-term investor's portfolio. ETFs make good sense for specific kinds of investors:

1. Older investors who use investments for their income. If you are older and need more income, but you would like to keep a significant allocation, ETFs dividends are a good choice. It doesn't matter how old an investor is, your portfolio needs to be age-appropriate with bonds and stocks along with dividend ETFs. This will let older investors do this while giving a steady stream of income.

2. Investors who would like to put money to work for them for a long period of time. If you would like to invest for five or more years, but you don't want to choose these individual stocks, dividend ETFs are a great choice.

3. Risk-averse investors use reliable dividends to help make a "price floor" to sort stock prices and use this to boost them during the tough times. If the stock market crashes, dividend stocks normally outperform their counterparts.

If any of the above sounds like you, then an ETF dividend would be a smart choice for you.

The Risks

You won't find any stock investment that doesn't come with a risk.

Investing in dividend stocks by going through ETFs can help you navigate the company and certain risks of investing in stocks. If you have a broad dividend ETF, and a company had a bad quarter, this effect on this investment will be minimal.

But you are still going to need to worry about the risks that don't have anything to do with systematic risks. If the whole market crashes, as it did in 2008 and 2009, your dividend ETFs will probably go down in value.

Another risk is interest rates. In an interest rate goes up, it will put pressure on every investment that generates an income, and this includes dividend stocks.

So, in summary, investing in ETF dividends will have risks, especially with short time periods. But it is still a great way to generate a stream of income, and with longer periods of time, there will be better returns.

Chapter 10: Enjoying The Rest of Your Life As a Rich Man

The main reason that most people invest is to have a safe retirement plan in place. The majority of most people's assets can be found in accounts that are dedicated especially toward that purpose, but as hard as saving enough money to have a comfortable retirement is, learning to live off your investment when you finally retire is just as hard.

Making a living from your dividends once you retire is a dream many people have, but only a handful achieve. In this day and age will all the rising life expectancies like the longest bull market and very low yielding bonds, people who want to retire face challenges from every aspect of life to create a constant stream of income that will last over your lifetime.

Before you zero in on one investment vehicle or strategy, you have to know how much risk you are willing to take when talking about your whole portfolio and your rate of return that you can reach.

Even though everybody will reach their own conclusions, we are connected through a certain desire. We want to have a specific quality of life during our retirement that allows us to sleep well and not to outlive our savings.

We all think that investing in dividends could help us achieve all of these objectives, but if your nest egg isn't large enough to let you live off that income without having to touch the principal, it is necessary to keep some sources that can easily be diversified.

Most of the paychecks you get during retirement get funded by a combination of withdrawals from your principal and investment incomes. Income generators like systematic withdrawals or annuities usually give you a better income than having a dividend strategy.

Being able to withdraw money takes a combination of selling stocks or funds and spending interest income to take care of the rest. The four percent rule for personal finances thrives here. The four percent rule tries to give you a stream of income while keeping a balance that allows money to be withdrawn for many years to come. What if I told you there was a different way to get that four percent without having to reduce principal or selling shares?

A way you can enhance your income is by investing in mutual funds and stocks that pay dividends. With time, the cash that gets generated by those payments will be able to supplement your pension income and Social Security, and it could give you all the money you are going to need to keep up the lifestyle that you are used to. You can live by only using your dividends as long as you do some planning.

Dividend Growth

The main reason why stocks need to be part of your portfolio is that stock dividends will grow with time. That growth can outpace inflation. For investors that have a long timeline, this could be exploited to carte portfolios that could be used just for living off dividend income.

The best strategy is to use those dividends to purchase more shares of a firm so you can get more dividends and purchase more shares.

Let's say you have invested $300,000 in Treasury bonds and another $500,000 in stocks that yield you three percent; this gives you $15,000 in dividend income every year. Once you have spent all of your dividends and you sell part of your bonds, you will finally reach the $40,000 you need for your annual income. After 21 years, your portfolio is going to be completely depleted.

Over that amount of time, your annual income could have gone up by another third to come to $20,000 a year, and this is after you have taken into consideration the amount of inflation. The most important thing here is that you still own all your stocks.

The mix of stocks and bonds are going to vary as based on how much of a nest egg you have, how tolerant you are of the market, and your objectives about returns, creating a portfolio with a couple of dozen good dividend stocks that yield no less than three percent and they increase their dividend by 3.5 percent every year can be extremely attainable.

Some people who have retired with a systemic withdrawal plan could end up feeling pressured to reduce their spending whenever the stock market is going through a decline; you could still enjoy a decent pay raise if you have the right stocks.

You Have Already Retired

Compounding income is great as long as you have a timeline that is long term, but what if you are going into retirement now? For investors, dividend growth and a higher yield just might do the trick.

For investors who have retired and want to live off just, their dividends might want to up their yield. Securities and stocks that have a higher yield normally don't generate a lot of distribution growth. You can add these to your portfolio, and it would increase your yield. This will go a long way in helping you pay your bills.

Investors who have retired don't need to stay away from stocks such as Proctor and Gamble. Firms that have higher dividend growth will increase income near or greater than the rates of inflation. This can help up your income for your future. When you add these firms to your portfolio, investors will sacrifice some of their current yield for a bigger pay in the future.

An investor who has a small portfolio might have problems living completely off their dividends, but the steady and rising payment will help reduce their principal withdrawals.

Most withdrawal methods involve a combination of the interest income from bonds and asset sales. There are other ways to hit that four percent rule. If you can invest in quality dividend stocks that have payouts that will increase, both new and older investors could benefit from a stock's inflations beating, compounding, distribution growth. You just need to do some planning, and you might just be able to live off your payments.

Companies that Pay Dividends

In order to alleviate worrying about all the ups and downs of the stock market, find companies that will pay a safe a growing dividend. You should focus on growing your income through dividends instead of all that noise caused by volatile stock prices. This works better if you have created an investment strategy, and you have gotten rid of your emotional risk that comes along with investing.

While a portfolio of stocks can experience some variables in market value, that income from your portfolio can constantly grow with time. Even while going through a financial crisis, there are about 230 companies that will still increase their dividend.

This is in strict contrast with the systematic withdrawal system. Which one of these sounds a lot more stressful:

- A person who lives off of the cash that is distributed and produced by investment every month

- A person who has to choose which assets to sell just to get enough money to live through the year

Living on income from dividends gives you money without you having to stress over trying to figure out what to sell and especially when there is another crash in the market.

Your focus stays on finding safe dividend payments instead of being concerned about the market's volatility and how this will impact how much you can withdraw. If there isn't a reduction in the dividend, the money will continue to roll in no matter the way the market might be.

Another good benefit of having stocks that offer dividends during retirement is most companies will increase their dividend rates with time, and this can help offset inflation.

The past performance of the stock market doesn't indicate future results. Those who need a decent size income will be able to protect their future with the correct stocks.

Having a strategy will grow and preserve your principal with time, which is very different than most withdrawal and annuity strategies. This gives you the chance to have something for your family. Investing in dividends will give you the flexibility to sell things if you were to need some money for something special or unexpected. Annuities don't have this kind of flexibility.

Dividend stocks have helped the market with time. They play an important role in capital growth and preservation. What exactly does this mean? Let's say you bought two $10,000 stocks on the S&P 500 in 1960. One of your investments didn't have any dividends. One's value was totally driven by the market.

The other investment had dividends that were paid by S&P companies. All payments were placed back into a stock once received. This helped them reach over $2.5 million by the close of 2017. The first investment only grew to $500,000. This shows that dividends do matter.

The importance of dividends will change with each decade. It all depends on how strong the market. During times when the stock market is stagnating, like during the 70s and 2000s, dividends had a larger part of the market's return.

Since the market is trading at a higher level today, which makes it harder to get capital gains, during the next decade, the market's return will be made up of dividends.

Stocks will always be more attractive than bonds, no matter the way you view it. The world of finance has undergone a lot of change during the past 40 years. You will no longer see double-digit yields on bonds. Most stocks will yield a lot more than bonds now.

Warren Buffett said back in May of 2018: "Long-term bonds are a terrible investment at current rates and anything close to current rates."

Why all the hatred for long-term bonds? Just like anything else, it is simple math. Long-term bonds will yield about a three percent rate today. This investment is taxable. This makes their after-tax yield around two and a half percent.

The Federal Reserve is getting about two percent annually for inflations. This makes the bonds after-tax return at only a half percent each year.

Bonds at this rate are completely ridiculous. When you think about the stock return at almost ten percent each year, dividends will increase their payments.

Other than fueling returns, investing in dividends has less volatility than other stocks, too.

Stocks that give dividend payments will have attributes that most conservative investors will like. They have a dividend that grows steadily, and that shows that the company is confident, stable, and durable.

To be able to pay out dividends, the company has to create a profit above and beyond the needs of the business. They are more careful about how they spend their money.

These qualities disqualify most of the lower quality businesses that have a lot of debt, weak cash flow, and volatile earnings. These characteristics could lead to huge losses and swings in the price of their shares.

Because these stocks have a lower volatility profile, they are more attractive to people who want to preserve more of their capital.

Hanging onto stocks instead of mutual funds or ETFs can protect all the money that you need to get while you remain in control of all your assets.

When you invest in securities on your own, it gets rid of the fees accumulated every year by most of the mutual funds and ETFs. This can save you thousands of dollars. All you will pay is a commission fee of about ten dollars for each trade if you go through a discount broker.

Managing your portfolio takes discipline and time. This is what makes it unacceptable for most people. Even though it doesn't guarantee that it will perform better, it will get rid of a huge drag on your return, and that is the fees that most advisors and managers on Wall Street will charge you.

High fees equal lower dividend incomes. The fees that most fund managers charge are the main reason why Warren Buffett always advises a normal person that if they want the best long-term results, they need to put their money into low-cost funds.

You might have heard about low-cost ETF's that only have a fee of around 0.1 percent. If you don't have the stomach or time to purchase and hang on to these stocks, it would be in your best interest to look at these for your portfolio.

The downside is you lose a wonderful benefit, which is control.

Most ETFs will own dozens, and possibly thousands of stocks. Some of these might be great businesses, and their dividends are safe, but others might be a lower quality and decide to get rid of them. Some might give you extremely high yields, while others won't generate any income at all.

Basically, this is saying that an ETF is many companies that might or might not match your income needs and will risk their tolerance extremely well.

Some ETFs found problems in the middle of the financial crisis since they weren't focused on the safety of their dividends. Their dividend income dropped by about 25 percent, and it took them several years to recover completely.

Choosing your own stocks while remaining focused on the safety of your income could deliver a faster-growing, higher income that is predictable as compared to the majority of the ETFs that are low cost. This helps you understand your investments, and this will help you handle the dips in the market with better confidence.

Owning dividend stocks for your retirement has many benefits. You will preserve your principal. Your income will stay steady no matter where the stock prices go. You will be able to protect how much you purchase with your dividend growth. The initial investment fee is going to be lower. You are going to know exactly what you have to pay.

But there are some risks that you should be aware of when you want to live off of the income from your dividends.

The Risks

The correct diversification is the best part of constructing your portfolio. If someone only buys dividend stocks for their retirement, they are only concentrating on one investment style and class. Most people will advise you to keep 20 and 75 percent exposure for your portfolio with cash and bonds, making up the remaining.

Allocating assets will depend upon your situation and what your risk tolerance is. The main objective for retirement is making sure that you keep your standard of living so that you don't end up outliving your money.

Some people will be able to meet this income amount through guaranteed interest from CDs, Social Security, and pension income. For these people, some investors might allow between 80 and 100 percent of their portfolio to be stocks that pay dividends in order to increase their income and to reach a stronger income growth capital appreciation. The mixture of your assets of cash, stocks, and bonds will be driven by how tolerant you are for risks and the income you need to live on.

Even though this goes against normal asset allocation, this calls for holding a balance of bonds and stocks. Most retired people look at their pension and Social Security as their "guaranteed" income. This makes them comfortable to invest in heavier stocks.

High-quality stocks can take up the volatility of your portfolio as compared to having a mixture of stocks and treasuries. This allows you to generate more income. This income will then increase faster. This allows your portfolio to have a larger potential for appreciating capital.

The short term returns are going to be less predictable. This can end up being an issue if you have to sell part of your portfolio at times just to make ends meet once you are retired. A zero return on bonds will be more attractive if your portfolio drops by just 25 percent.

You could also get into trouble if you only have high-yielding stocks that are concentrated in a few sectors, such as utilities and real estate. You could also be affected by hindsight bias. People who are constantly wanting to own dividends that grow have caused stock groups to become hugely popular with investors.

These stocks get more attention from investors since they can outperform the market, and people like assuming many will continue to grow and pay their dividends, which isn't a guarantee. Look at AIG or GE before the financial crisis to get an example.

These two companies aren't alone. Companies that are a part of the S&P 500 lowered their dividends by about 24 percent between 2008 and 2010. The index fell by about 22 percent. They outperformed the market, but they still took a huge hit as compared to bonds.

It is important to diversify your holding and own stocks rather than bonds. If a company can't pay its debts, it will file for bankruptcy. If things were to get rough for a company, it would get rid of the dividends first in order to stay afloat. Basically, this is saying that their dividend income and stocks are riskier than bonds. You won't ever find a free lunch.

Only focusing on the return of income is another trap that some investors fall into. If a company can pay its dividend doesn't automatically make them a better investment. It doesn't matter if your money comes from selling parts of your portfolio, bonds, or dividend income.

A lot of people prefer to keep their principals untouched and live off only the income our dividends generate every month, even if this does give less of a return. This is irrational and can cause you to chase higher-yielding stocks. It would be a huge mistake to buy stocks that match your objective.

Most stocks that have a yield higher than five percent are showing you that something might be wrong with a business, or they could end up cutting the dividend in order to help the company survive. With problems like this, the principal will face the biggest risk of facing long-term erosion.

You need to figure out why the company offers large payouts. We think that investors should find low-risk stocks that give five percent or less. These usually have better chances of growing and maintaining the principal and earnings with time.

It doesn't matter because the reality is that most people who retire can't live off of the dividends every year without using some of their capital. These people need to try to create a portfolio for a complete return instead of income alone.

After you have figured out your portfolio, you can find out the amount of cash flow you will get from it, whether it is through selling assets, dividends, payments from interest, or other things. Payments from dividends are just one way to create a constant cash flow, but this should not be seen as a vacuum. You should always keep an open mind and make sure you stay aware of different income sources that could be a better fit.

Some other downsides with investing is the time it can take to remain current in holdings and the knowledge that is needed to get you started. Investing isn't rocket science; you do need a stomach for risk, and enough literacy to know the basics of a company, common sense, and a commitment to remain current with your holdings.

If you were to look at the savings you receive from being a do-it-yourself investor versus an investor who handles your money for a fee, you could save thousands of dollars if you are willing to make a commitment. This could end up helping you in the long run with retirement, and it beats having to work if investing is something you like better.

This also assumes that an investor is able to find stocks that are safe and will perform well and ETFs that are available.

Dealing with your assets and getting ready to retire is an overwhelming process. There are a lot of different decisions that must be made based on risk, life expectations, and objectives. These differences can drive the decisions you make, but you can rush them.

For every decision you make, you have to review all of the fine print, flexibility, and fees of the stock. You need to remember that you need a constant cash flow, and you have tied yourself down to one source like dividend income, annuity payments, or bond interest.

Quality stocks can give you a foundation of income and a complete return for most portfolios. Most investors don't have a huge nest egg that they need to live off of during retirement, but having a properly created portfolio of stocks could give you long-term capital appreciation, income growth, and a safe income to help you make a larger portfolio last the rest of your life.

FAQs

- Are there tax advantages for owning ETFs?

Just like conventional mutual index funds, the majority of ETFs try to stay on track with an index like the S&P 500. An ETF will only sell and buy stocks when the benchmark index does. Large investment moves, such as if a company gets taken away from the index, occurs rarely.

Plus, ETF managers will use the losses to help offset their gains. This will reduce or get rid of the taxable gains that the shareholders get at the end of every year.

- Do ETFs have dividend distributions and capital gains? If they do, can these be reinvested?

ETFs, distribute capital gains just like mutual funds do. This normally happens in December. The dividends get paid quarterly or monthly. It all depends on the EFT. It's rare for index ETFs to have capital gains, and you might face taxes even if you didn't sell any shares.

You might be able to reinvest your dividends, and capital gains it all depends on who you have your ETFs with.

- Why is an ETFs market price different from their net asset value?

The market price of ETFs is controlled by supply and demand. It all depends on market forces. The price might be below or above the NAV, which is called the discount or premium.

If you want to find out information on a certain ETFs closing price, look for the tab called "Price and Performance" on your ETFs profile page.

- How does an ETFs market price get determined?

An ETF's market price gets determined by the bonds and stocks' prices that are owned by the ETF along with the supply and demand of the market.

A market price can end up changing during the day and could end up being below or above the full price of what is in the ETF. These differences are normally quite small; it might be significant if the market is volatile.

- Are there certain kinds of ETFs that I can place?

You have the ability to place any kind of trade just like you do with stocks, and these include:

- o Stop-limit orders: these have multiple steps. This will require a trigger price. If the price moves past the price you picked, the order will be created automatically.

- o Stop orders: these also have multiple steps. You have to set a trigger price, and if that price moves past that trigger price, the market order automatically gets created.

- o Market orders: these will usually go right away at the best price available, but you won't have as much control over the price you will get or pay.

- o Limit orders: this ensures that you will get the price in the range that you have set. This will be the minimum you will accept or the max you will pay.

- What is the difference between a mutual fund and an ETF?

There are a lot more similarities than differences between mutual funds and ETFs. The largest differences are:

1. ETFs pricing is more transparent. They give you real-time pricing so that you will be able to see the change in prices during the day. Mutual funds aren't priced until after the close of the day. This means you aren't going to know the price until after the trade has been placed.

2. ETFs will have lower minimums. The minimum of an ETF is the price of one share. This might be as low as $50. It all depends on the ETF. Mutual funds might require you to pay anything from $1,000 to $3,000 or even higher.

Conclusion

Thank you for making it through to the end of *Retire Early with ETF Investing Strategy*, let's hope it was informative and able to provide you with all of the tools you need to achieve your goals whatever they may be.

The next step is to start looking at your current financial situation and figure out what your goals are for the future. As you have heard time and time again, investing and retirement won't look the same for two people. It is ultimately up to you how you decide to use your money and what to do to make sure you are able to retire as early as you want to. Once you have figured out your goals and you know where you stand financially, you can start to take some active steps towards making more money and saving more for your retirement. I would suggest getting into investing before you try to branch out into bigger things like real estate and the like. It also wouldn't hurt to check to see if you could be making more at your job and if you are using your time and money wisely there. In the end, find what works best for you and feels right. It's your life and your retirement.

Finally, if you found this book useful in any way, a review on Amazon is always appreciated!

www.ingramcontent.com/pod-product-compliance
Lightning Source LLC
Chambersburg PA
CBHW060952050726
47592CB00003B/1199